Fabian Society
11 Dartmouth Street
London SW1H 9BN
www.fabians.org.uk

Fabian ideas
Editorial Director: Tom Hampson

First published 2007

ISBN 978 0 7163 0621 4

British Library Cataloguing in Publication data.
A catalogue record for this book is available from the British Library.

Printed and bound by Bell & Bain, Glasgow

The Fabian Society

The Fabian Society is Britain's leading left of centre think tank and
political society, committed to creating the political ideas and policy
debates which can shape the future of progressive politics.

With over 300 Fabian MPs, MEPs, Peers, MSPs and AMs, the Society
plays an unparalleled role in linking the ability to influence policy
debates at the highest level with vigorous grassroots debate among our
growing membership of over 7000 people, 70 local branches meeting
regularly throughout Britain and a vibrant Young Fabian section
organising its own activities. Fabian publications, events and ideas
therefore reach and influence a wider audience than those of any
comparable think tank. The Society is unique among think tanks in
being a thriving, democratically-constituted membership organisation,
affiliated to the Labour Party but organisationally and editorially
independent.

For over 120 years Fabians have been central to every important
renewal and revision of left of centre thinking. The Fabian commitment
to open and participatory debate is as important today as ever before
as we explore the ideas, politics and policies which will define the next
generation of progressive politics in Britain, Europe and around the
world. Find out more at **www.fabians.org.uk**

Joining the Fabians is easy
For more information about joining the Fabian Society and to learn
more about our recent publications, please turn to **page 30**.

Stronger Together
The 21st century case for Scotland and Britain

by Gordon Brown
and Douglas Alexander

FABIAN SOCIETY

About the authors

Gordon Brown is MP for Kirkcaldy and Cowdenbeath and Chancellor of the Exchequer. He was born in 1951 and was educated in Kirkcaldy. He studied at Edinburgh University from the age of 16 gaining an honours degree and Doctorate of Philosophy. He was elected Rector of Edinburgh University by the student body and from 1972 to 1975 was Chairman of the University Court. From 1976 to 1980, he lectured at Edinburgh University and then Glasgow College of Technology, before taking up a current affairs post at STV. From 1983 he was Chair of the Labour Party Scottish Council and in May 1983 became MP for Dunfermline East. He was Opposition spokesperson on Treasury and Economic Affairs (Shadow Chancellor) from 1992. With the election of the Labour government in May 1997, he became Chancellor of the Exchequer and is now the longest serving Chancellor for 200 years.

Douglas Alexander is MP for Paisley and Renfrewshire South and Secretary of State for Transport and Secretary of State for Scotland. He was born in Glasgow in 1967 and was educated in Scotland and Canada, going on to study at Edinburgh University and the University of Pennsylvania. He worked as a lawyer prior to entering Parliament in 1997. He was Minister of State for Europe from May 2005-May 2006, Minister for Trade, Investment and Foreign Affairs from September 2004-April 2005 and Minister for e-Commerce and Competitiveness at the Department for Trade and Industry in June 2001. In May 2002 he moved to the Cabinet Office, becoming Minister for the Cabinet Office in June 2003 where, among other things, he led on the Government's better regulation agenda, public and civil service reform and e-government.

Acknowledgments

The authors would like to thank Maggie Vaughan, Wendy Alexander, John McLaren, Paul Sinclair and Tom Hampson for all their hard work and advice in helping produce this pamphlet.

Gordon Brown at the Fabian New Year Conference 2007 *Empics*

Contents

Stronger Together

Introduction

This modernised Union has radically different characteristics from the one of 1707. In modern Scotland we have deeper and stronger family ties with England than at any time in our history. And the links which connect the Scottish economy to the rest of the UK are deeper, more complex and more productive than at any time in the last three hundred years.

This modern Union is not founded just on institutions as it was in the past, but is now based on shared values and a shared vision of the society we want to create, one where social justice is more important than borders. In a world which is becoming smaller, a world of endless diversity where boundaries and borders are coming down finding a common purpose which still allows a distinctive identity to flourish within a greater community is key.

Finding a common identity which gives us the unity to prosper in harmony, but which does not demand a homogenized identity. Stressing those values that provide bridges between communities so that we can advance together for the common good. These are advances that make the UK a model for countries that continue the recognition of cultural identities with cooperation and cohesion.

This is a requirement that will become even more important to the new mobile societies that will characterise the next stage of the global economy. Far from Scotland's relationship with the UK being an anachronism, getting the balance right between diversity and

1

common bonds and shared values can be the shape of global things to come.

Starting from these principles – that no nation can be aloof or isolated and all will have to seek alliances for their future welfare – the United Kingdom with a UK parliament and devolved arrangements for Scotland, Wales and Northern Ireland looks more in tune with modernity than most.

It is by showing our identity is based not on race or ethnicity but on shared values that we best ensure that in a society of many different people with diverse interests there are ties that bind and thus integration.

And if Nationalists do believe that there can be Scots of many different colours and creeds bound by common values, they have to explain why those common values are halted at the border with England, when in truth modern Britain itself is founded on that common ground of shared values.

The alternative to today's cooperation is the old Nationalist retreat from engagement. Yet it is clear to us that far from the links being weaker than ever before our interdependence is today even greater than before and it makes us stronger.

The desire of Nationalists to swim against the tide of globalisation and interdependence shows they look at the world through 19th and 20th century eyes. Denied their two old pillars – Scotland refused devolution at London's hands and Scotland suffering economic deprivation at London's hands – the Nationalists are left only with a politics of girning grudge and manufactured grievance.

That their complaints have no purchase on reality is shown by how their grudges and grievances have shifted over time. In the 1950s and 1960s before oil, whisky was supposed to be the key to Scotland's prosperity. Scots were right not to bet on that one – whisky, while important to us, is now less than one per cent of our economy.

In the 1970s the SNP argument was founded on oil wealth. Now in the 21st century no modern economy would base its whole future on just one commodity and one as volatile in price. Indeed now the global challenge is to find alternatives to oil.

First the SNP future was to withdraw from Europe. That changed to independence in Europe. Now they have walked away from Europe as their best argument and are reduced to cherry picking statistics from other small nations in an attempt to assert that 'small is beautiful'.

The simple truth is that Scotland earns more from trading with England than from trade within our own country. More than that, Scotland's trade with England dwarfs our trade with the rest of the world. To break up the Union as the Nationalists wish is to jeopardise our financial stability.

The connections we have with England are central to our economic success. The prosperity and well-being of our neighbour and biggest trading partner has an enormous bearing on our own well-being. A prosperous England gives Scotland – and Wales and Northern Ireland – greater economic opportunities in a growing market in which to trade.

The UK Government is providing the stability of a macroeconomic framework which is delivering prosperity. As other countries equip themselves for global challenges, Scotland cannot afford to sink into the morass of a constitutional crisis.

A better future is one which recognises our interdependencies and the contribution we can all make to the common good and results that flow from it – the best opportunity of achieving a more just society.

Ties that bind

I t is said in our country that the first five hundred years of any institution's history are always the most difficult. In 2007, the Union of Scotland and England has lasted a mere three hundred years – so we might think of the issues between the nations simply as growing pains.

Devolution has certainly been the most radical rebuilding of the Union in that time. Scottish identity has been rightly re-affirmed and the Scottish commitment to social justice given a new, dynamic way to express itself through the Scottish Parliament.

The focus of Scottish life has shifted more towards Holyrood. But that should not be allowed to mask the fact that the links which bind Britain together have continued to deepen since devolution and have strengthened rather than withered. Family ties, economic ties and indeed values are stronger now than before.

Family ties

Ask a Scottish family today if they have any relatives south of the border and you'll get a remarkable answer which contradicts the common view that Scotland and England are moving apart not closer together.

In 1707 when Scotland joined England only 30,000 of people living in Scotland had English relatives. Even in 1910 fewer than

800,000 had English family links. Today, around two and a half million Scottish residents are either English themselves or have relatives who are English. That means that for the first time ever almost half of Scots have relatives from south of the border.

And the traffic is far from one way. More than 410,000 of the Scottish population were born in England – almost one in twelve of the people living in Scotland was born south of the border. And nearly twice that number of Scots – 795,000 – now live in England and Wales. That means almost one in six people born in Scotland chooses to live in another part of Britain.

Indeed, the recent survey by HBOS revealed that millions of people migrate from one part of the United Kingdom to another. In a nine year period almost half a million Scots have moved to other parts of the UK, more than half a million have come to Scotland.

That record migration is made so much easier because of the close and ever closer ties there are between the constituent parts of the UK.

We talk of Scotland's American connections, Australian connections, New Zealand connections, Canadian connections and South African. All these connections are important to us, showing that Scots are global in reach and outlook. But no country has stronger family connections with Scotland than England.

At the time of the Act of Union only three per cent of Scots had relatives in England. People will ask what sense it makes today to break up that Union when half the population now have relatives in England.

What would that mean to families north and south of the border? Nearly 800,000 Scots in England and more than 400,000 Englishmen and women in Scotland would have to choose which passport to hold. Two and a half million Scots would have to call their relatives foreigners.

Values that bind us together

You have to ask why these relationships have been formed in the first place. These are not just random marriage patterns. What they speak to is deep and deepening connections between the nations of Britain in many other senses too. Families are not just built on marriage ceremonies – they also represent shared values.

So many Scots would not make their homes south of the border (and English people north of it) if they did not feel comfortable that they will be living in a place which they could call home – communities which shared their values, their hopes and their aspirations.

And what these family links also speak to are the economic opportunities and ties between our nations which give individuals the chance to advance.

Increasingly modern Britain is a country based on shared values and on social justice. In previous centuries the values that bind us together were never as clear as they are now. In our country a commitment to liberty for all only evolved over the course of three centuries.

Equally, in our country, a belief in social responsibility shared by all – the moral sense that Adam Smith and David Hume talked about – only recently became central to how we think about society.

It is only in the 20th century we can genuinely say that our country is founded on the idea of fairness to all. These are values that brought us together to build a National Health Service founded by the Welshman Nye Bevan, in a Government led by a Londoner – Clem Attlee – and with strong Scottish support. That is why we have health care free at the point of delivery in every corner of the land – the embodiment of fairness to all.

In the 19th century, John Stuart Mill observed that the elements that defined a nation were not just the desire on the part of the inhabitants to be governed together but the 'common sympathy' instilled by shared history, values and language.

"Free institutions", he wrote, "are next to impossible in a country made up of different nationalities. Among a people without fellow feeling, especially if they read and speak different languages, the united public opinion, necessary to the working of representative government, cannot exist."

'Sympathy' was the word Adam Smith used to describe what we had in common, even if in 1603 it might just have been a joint monarch, and in 1707 a common Parliament.

Yet over the years much has changed and today it is not simply that we share a common island, and a common language, but that we also share what John Stuart Mill agreed is a commitment to openness and internationalism, to public service and to justice, to creativity and inventiveness, to democracy and tolerance.

This sense of common purpose has carried on for centuries. In the industrial age it was taken on by early trade unionists, the founders of the Labour movement, workers educational associations, the co-operative movement. The trade union movement has played a historic role in Scotland and many Scottish leaders became British leaders, not because of their accent or birth place, but precisely because they believed in a strong sense of community and social responsibility.

And again, if Nationalists are not persuaded by the moral argument or by a sense of justice which moved Scottish trade unionists to join with their British comrades in the fight for rights, then let it be put this way.

Poorly paid workers, with few rights and bad conditions in England would have a direct effect on investment jobs and prosperity north of the border and *vice versa*.

Scots, English, Welsh and Irish trade unionists realised what the Nationalists do not – that solidarity and the improvement of pay and conditions throughout the UK was the only way of improving the job prospects of workers throughout the nations and regions of Britain.

This sense of common purpose inspired generations of men and women who did not allow liberty to descend into a selfish individualism or into a crude libertarianism. These were men and women who, as is the essence of the Labour movement, chose solidarity in preference to selfishness, thereby creating the Scotland and Britain of civic responsibility, civic society and the public realm.

This is the Britain we admire. The Britain of thousands of voluntary associations, of mutual societies, craft unions, insurance and friendly societies and co-operatives, of churches and faith groups, of municipal provision from libraries to parks, and the Britain of public service.

Mutuality, co-operation, civic associations, social responsibility and a strong civic society, are all concepts that after a moment's thought we see clearly have always owed most to progressive opinion in British life and thought.

The Scottish way is always at the core of British history, championing the ideas of 'active citizenship', 'good neighbour', civic pride and the public realm.

These are not the values of yesteryear but modern values upon which modernised Britain is based. And they reflect the shared values of the peoples of Britain. A YouGov survey showed that as many as 90 per cent of British people thought that fairness and fair play were important in defining Britishness.

Ninety per cent of British people think the NHS portrays a positive symbol of the real Britain, founded on the core value of fairness and the belief that everyone should have access to health care founded on their need, not on their ability to pay.

And, according to one survey, more than 70 per cent of British people pride ourselves in all three qualities – our tolerance, responsibility and fairness together. These are modern values, but they are not new. They are Scottish values but also English values – the values of the whole of Britain.

And how do we express these values in Britain? What difference do they make to national life?

We pool and share our resource because we believe that if the strong help the weak it makes us all stronger. That is the principle which underpins both our system of National Insurance and in the allocation of public expenditure.

In other countries, citizenship carries understandings about rights and responsibilities. Social insurance is a concept that is more admired in theory than today practised in reality, but British citizenship is still reinforced by the powerful and widely held idea that as citizens of Britain we all contribute to the social protection against sickness, incapacity and widowhood and towards the pensions of each other.

And it is the very sharing of risks over our 60 million people that maximises the rights of citizenship. British National Insurance is a sharing of risks by all of us that provides rights for each of us, guaranteeing provision for any insured family or citizen in any part of Britain.

Of course, the British idea of national insurance has changed over time and will continue to change. But no one can deny that the sharing of risks among all our citizens is a more potent support for the poor and thus for social justice than the sharing of risks among five million Scots.

So the sum is greater than its parts. We gain from our interdependence and would be diminished without it. The interests of Scots, English and Welsh are not in conflict with each other, but dependent upon each other.

And those values and family ties are reinforced by the deep and deepening economic links between Scotland and England.

Economic ties

Scotland's largest trading partner has long been England – and through the United Kingdom it is a true partnership. Goods and services are not just sold to another country, they are bought by a neighbour with whom we have strong links. And those links mean that in ten out of eleven standard industry sectors Scotland has more trade with the rest of the United Kingdom than with the rest of the world put together.

This is not a legacy of the past but a clear sign of how our economy is responding to current challenges and the challenges of the future. And the way to social justice through full employment and prosperity is trade not isolation. As Scotland's economy has changed – and it has radically – so have our markets. They have deepened. Today those traditional industries that we think of as Scottish play a smaller role than they did in our economy. Fishing, for example, accounts for just 0.3 per cent of the economy. Mining, including coal and quarrying, is also just 0.3 per cent while spirits, including the whole whisky industry, is at 1.3 per cent. Metal and metal products accounts for just 1.3 per cent, and shipbuilding, including all transport equipment, is only 0.9 per cent.

But new industries are taking their place and the English market is key to their growth. Take financial services which is now 7 per cent of our economy – seven times the size of shipbuilding, six times whisky and spirits and metals, and 25 times mining and fishing. And employment levels reflect that while there are 5,600 people employed in fishing, 8,400 in shipbuilding, 7,800 in whisky, there are now 118,700 in financial services. On average in the last six years financial services has had an annual growth rate of 8.1 per cent. The banking sector has grown even faster at 8.5 per cent a year.

But the strength of the Scottish financial services industries comes from exports. £7.7 billion of the £9.5 billion financial services

11

generated are exported every year. Ninety two per cent of exports go to the rest of the UK, but only 8 per cent to the rest of the world.

Trade with the rest of the UK – almost entirely with England – is a bigger market for Scotland than all her trade with the rest of the world. In fact, it is almost twelve times bigger. Even when we look at the broader sector of financial and business services, the figure is 82 per cent of exports to the UK, just 18 per cent to the rest of the world. This trade is possible, of course, because we have a truly open single market in the UK and a successful single currency – a state the EU aspires to but has not yet reached.

Financial services are a Scottish success story which make us in Scotland rightly proud. But they are a success story because successful Scottish products are successfully sold to the whole of the rest of the UK. What the Nationalists won't admit is that in financial services – as with so many other industries – Scotland's economic networks have been built on a cross-Britain basis. These ties have not held us back but have been the key to growth.

Our top financial service companies employ English as well as Scottish executives. They have weight because of their influence throughout the whole of the UK. In other words the companies are connected by takeovers, mergers and alliances built on a UK-wide basis. Once severed, these critical connections could never be restored. Separation would destroy one of the key bases of our comparative advantage.

Scotland, with her partners in the UK, has built these networks over 300 years and when they have become central to the growth process people have to think twice about severing them.

And what would happen if we decided to cut them? The SNP cannot explain their financial services policy. Britain has one financial services regulator – the FSA. Under a separate Scotland the same financial services companies would have to report to two separate regulators. Being subject to two regulatory regimes would make investors think twice and discourage new investment in Scotland.

No comfort is to be found in resorting to the old claim that Europe will solve the problem – European integration is insufficiently advanced for a single regulator to be agreed. And besides what we sell to the English market in financial services is more than 11 times greater than our sales to the rest of the world. More money is generated for Scotland through trade with England in just financial services than from the trade we have in all sectors in all areas across the whole of the European Union, indeed the whole of the 27 European states.

The SNP say setting monetary and fiscal policy in London has been, at best, "inappropriate" and, at worst, "positively damaging" for Scotland. Scotland, they have continually argued, could enjoy lower interest rates with its own separate currency. For decades they have proposed the creation of a Scottish pound and thus a Scottish monetary policy system that would set interest rates in Scotland. However they also say they want to join the euro, which would mean other countries would make that decision.

But in recent months their policy has descended into confusion and often farce. The leader Alex Salmond said they would stick with the Bank of England. Then he said they would still have a separate Scottish monetary policy authority. Then they said they would follow the arrangements of Ireland after the 1920s, or those of Australia (where there was effectively no independent currency for years and instead many currencies operated simultaneously at the turn of the last century).

At another point they have suggested they would follow the arrangements Belgium had with Luxembourg. This is a position of utter confusion in the areas where the needs of stability demand clarity. At one and the same time they seem to favour a Scottish pound (their official policy of the past); a British pound (but without the power to determine whether England would accept any monetary arrangement with an independent Scotland); and an English pound with a Scottish interest rate setting committee (which would be a recipe for the confusion that existed over the ERM).

It is however clear that under separate arrangements Scotland would have an instability-premium where interest rates would not be lower but higher as the result of the SNP's confusion and lack of credibility.

The Union is vital to our financial services – and Scotland's financial sector plays an important part in the UK economy. Half of our top ten companies – RBS, HBOS, Standard Life, Scottish Widows and Aegon – are in financial services and integrated into the UK market in terms of sales, activity and employment.

Edinburgh is a crucial financial centre but it also benefits from close links with the rest of the UK and, in particular, London. The SNP decry London as though it is in opposition to Scottish interests. But the truth is whatever constitutional path we go down London will remain one of the wealthiest hubs of international trade in the world. At the moment, through the Union, Scotland has influence in London. The Nationalists must explain – particularly if they see London as a rival – why it is in Scotland's interests to give up influence in one of the key cities in world trade.

In the UK, as in the new world shaped by globalisation, we communicate, connect and compete as never before. The stability and strength of the integrated UK economy is key to all sectors of the Scottish economy.

So there is a new 21st century economic argument for the Union. It is a vital and decisive argument which rests on the increasing importance of those connections, networks and links that will make the biggest and most successful industries even bigger and more successful in the future. These are connections that if strengthened enrich us; connections that if broken could easily impoverish us.

It is to Scotland's benefit that these links are nurtured not neglected. That is what this Government is doing with a partnership at Holyrood and Westminster. Jack McConnell's Financial Services Task Force is working with the Scottish industry on skills and training.

At the same time the Scottish Secretary sits on the Financial Services Task Force at Westminster to ensure that the views of the Scottish industry are voiced at a UK level.

Analysis of our financial services sector shows that increasingly, at the centre of and relying on the knowledge networks that bind the UK together, Scotland benefits from being part of the United Kingdom – connections, partnership, mutual support and flexibility going hand in hand.

Other countries may have managed their affairs in such a way that their separateness is the foundation of their economic base and activity. In Scotland's case it is the connections we have, with England in particular, that are central to our economic success and thus to jobs and incomes for our people and the achievement of our goals of full employment and prosperity for all.

In almost every sector of the economy trade with England is bigger than trade with the whole of the rest of the world.

Let us be clear: every country depends upon external trade. But Scotland depends on external trade more than almost any other country today.

Anyone who argues Scotland can underplay the importance of trade with the rest of Britain forgets that in key areas like manufacturing and finance and business services, exports to the rest of the UK are even larger than sales to the Scottish domestic market.

Our domestic markets are small and our external markets are large – a situation that will become even more important in the years to come. This shows, again, that our interdependence is greater. Our connections are stronger and more important than ever before. These are connections which enrich us, rather than impoverishing us, but which if broken could not be easily replaced.

So anyone who argues we can undervalue the rest of the UK in favour of the rest of the world forgets that in ten out of eleven standard industry sectors trade with the rest of the UK is a bigger market for Scotland than all her trade with the rest of the world. In heavy manufacturing it's 52 per cent, in electricity gas and water supply it's 98 per cent, in retail hotels and entertainment it's 81 per cent, in transport postage and communications it's 91 per cent, in business activities it's 75 per cent, and even in education it's 72 per cent.

These are the trading patterns that create jobs in an integrated economic area that we disrupt at our peril. Indeed companies headquartered in other parts of the UK account for almost a third of Scottish output. More importantly perhaps the fastest growing of the most dynamic sectors have the strongest links with England. Even more striking, these – the future wealth creators, the most dynamic sectors of the Scottish economy – all rely on ever-closer networks to share knowledge and ideas.

Scotland exports 2003	Exports £m		Share of total exports	
	UK	WORLD	UK	WORLD
Agriculture, forestry and fishing	540	190	74%	26%
Mining	1,299	448	74%	26%
Manufacturing	10,750	12,384	46%	54%
Energy and water	1,411	29	98%	2%
Construction	1,066	63	94%	6%
Distribution and catering	1,418	1,388	51%	49%
Transport and telecommunication	1,673	367	82%	18%
Finance and business	9,704	2,128	82%	18%
Public administration	7	2	75%	25%
Education, health and social work	401	150	73%	27%
Other Services	415	52	89%	11%
Total	28,684	17,201	63%	37%

Table 1   Exports from Scotland in 2003

Around the world, the patterns of production are changing with profound implications for the wealth of our nation in future years. With China and Asia becoming the low cost manufacturers of the future, UK economic value will be increasingly derived not so much from raw materials and physical production but from exploiting knowledge.

The nations that can thrive in a highly competitive global economy will be those that can compete on high technology and intellectual strength – attracting the highest-skilled people and the companies which have the potential to innovate and to turn innovation into commercial opportunity.

These are the sources of the new prosperity. A growing consensus is emerging that the key sources of future UK wealth will be, in addition to business and financial services:

- creative industries;
- pharmaceuticals, health care and life sciences;
- education services; and
- environmentally related industries.

The UK is well placed with its scientists amongst the most successful in the world. Despite representing only 1 per cent of the world's population, the UK undertakes 5 per cent of the world's science and has 12 per cent of all citations.

But the economic potential of science and innovation will be lost unless the business benefits of science are realised. The Government's Ten Year Science Engineering and Technology Plan recognised the importance of translating R&D into new business products and services in order to generate the economic opportunities which underpin economic growth.

Our creative industries are now a mainstream rather than marginal element of our economy. Design, advertising, music, film and TV, fashion, computer games and publishing produce a higher proportion of our total wealth than anywhere else in the world. UK firms register more trademarks and designs with the EU than any other country.

The global market value of the creative industries has increased from $831 billion in 2000 to $1.3 trillion in 2005 – more than 7 per cent of global GDP.

In the UK, KPMG predicts 46 per cent employment growth and 136 per cent output growth in the creative industries between 1995 and 2015. Between 1997 and 2004 the creative industries averaged 6 per cent growth, around twice the rate of the economy as a whole.

Far from being 'economy lite', our creative sectors should be seen as 'economy central'. We're the second largest exporter of television programmes in the world (after the USA).

Our computer software industry doubled their exports between 1997 and 2004. And our computer games industry now employs 22,000 people. It is clear therefore that our creative industries have a key role in supporting the UK's future wealth.

So, the opportunity is clear – these markets will continue to grow, and Britain is good at them. It is surely an achievable goal: to make Scotland and Britain the world's creative hub, building on Scotland's comparative advantage, derived from our ingenuity and inventiveness.

The creative industries depend on skills: for example, 33 per cent of women and 46 per cent of men used IT at work in 1993. Now it is 64 per cent and 65 per cent respectively. And this growth in creative industries is part of the modern tide which is seeing our economy demand greater skills and education. While in 1981, managerial, professional, and associate professional and technical occupations accounted for 26 per cent of jobs they will account for 40 per cent by 2008. In 1998 at SVO level 4 or above there are just 26 per cent in 1998, and in 2003 32 per cent. And it will be 35 per cent by 2008 – a 30 per cent increase.

And it follows on, therefore, that another sector that will succeed is education and science. The main driver of growth, wealth creation and employment across all industries is the production, use and dissemination of knowledge.

This makes the role of education and especially our universities key: traditionally praised for their teaching, now their research and innovation make them a vital hub of industry and the economy. This sector is another example beyond the financial services of the need for ever stronger partnerships. Sharing knowledge and ideas is the key to future success.

We need to recognise, also, that education accounts for 6.5 per cent of the Scottish economy today – a much higher share – and that education could become our biggest export. Our universities have become the workshops of the knowledge economy, production lines of ideas that are linked throughout the UK.

Look at the integrated networks which lie at the heart of Scottish universities' success today. Funded only 40 per cent by core grant – the rest comes from other official research and private sources.

With just 9 per cent of the UK population, Scotland:

- Wins 12 per cent of the total UK funding council resources for research.
- Wins 13 per cent of government research departments' research investment.
- Wins 12 per cent of the EU research resources spent in the UK.

Scottish universities succeed within a UK framework where the UK stands second only to America in the role of its universities in knowledge creation. Of the world's top 200 universities Britain has 24. Three of these are in Scotland – more than Ireland, Iceland and Norway combined. (Referred to by those who want separation as the 'northern arc of prosperity' we should be emulating!) The economic value of these relationships is becoming ever clearer, not just in their growing size but in the knowledge networks and the research relationships that Scotland must retain not sever.

Scottish universities generate 12 per cent of UK spin-out companies; grant 15 per cent of licenses and file 11 per cent of patents.

While the big American universities do more commercialisation than any UK universities, Scotland's efficiency is significantly better. Per £100 million spent on research, Scottish universities produce five times as many spin-outs, 50 per cent more licenses and almost three times as many disclosures.

For every £1 million spent on research, Scottish universities generate £32,250 in royalty income compared with £29,380 in America. This is the basis of knowledge creation that will serve the Scottish economy well. In the future, Scotland benefiting not from the isolation of Scottish universities but from their pre-eminence as part of a UK system.

This research base in our universities is the life support system for Scotland's life sciences industry. This is one of the newest industries of the future. In Scotland over 550 organisations are engaged in life sciences, employing more than 26,500 people.

Scotland is already home to 15 per cent of the UK's life sciences companies. But again research in life sciences depends on extensive collaboration and connections. So we disrupt their networks at our peril. Quite simply the application of knowledge critically depends upon flows of knowledge within and between economies.

Networks and partnerships are the connections through which knowledge flows. But such networks – as with many formal and informal institutions – are not the immediate result of a policy or political direction. They are an outcome of history and develop through time. And so there has been a marked increase in the indicators of international integration and connectedness such as cross-border ownership of inventions, international co-operation in science and technology; rising proportion of scientific publications with foreign co-authors; rising percentage of patents with foreign co-inventors; rising international mobility of students and workers.

So what does this mean for Scotland's future growth potential and its economic ties to the rest of the UK?

Scotland's interconnectedness with the rest of the UK allows it to have a comparative advantage in the development of future knowledge-based activities that rely upon underlying networks. And this isn't theory, it is happening now.

It is the path we must follow in the future if we are to succeed. These connections, networks and knowledge flows are a product of our shared history. They cannot simply be replicated on a whim. But they can be destroyed by constitutional change such as independence.

To demonstrate the power of networks in disseminating knowledge, consider another example: Europe and the United States. The European Union cannot in the short-term match the United States as an integrated economy even if there is a free flows of goods, services, and factors of production across Europe. This is because the US has had more than 200 years of the development of social and economic networks that cannot be created in Europe over night.

Scotland, with her partners in the UK, has built these knowledge networks over 300 years and it would be folly to sever them just at the point where they have become central to the growth process.

What a Nationalist position will be reluctant to face up to is that Scotland's networks in the key areas – science, medicine, financial services, life sciences, energy – have been built on a cross-UK basis. Those who have for two decades advocated 'independence in Europe', contend that Scotland, removed from the UK, can substitute membership of the EU for the Union.

It is true that Scotland could enter a free trading area within the EU. But those who make this case have ignored the impact of separation on the networks that are becoming increasingly important to economic development.

In short, a severed Scotland would lose the network benefits and social capital that have been built up since 1707. Separation would destroy one of the key bases of our comparative advantage because of the loss of UK network benefits.

Recently Anne Glover, Scotland's New Chief Scientific Adviser noted: "In centuries past, science was an individual pursuit. It was a lot easier to take a discovery and identify a main person who was responsible for it. Nowadays, in almost every area of research, we rely on team-working. That's the way science is going."

In Scotland that team work she talks about is organised on a UK-wide basis. Take Dundee University and the teams at Dundee working on their four major life sciences projects funded by the Medical Research Council, Wellcome, Cancer Research UK and international partners from the pharmaceutical industry.

All the leading scientists involved in these projects are initially from outside Scotland but have made their family homes, their careers and their futures in Dundee. Some have brought with them research teams who have relocated in Scotland from elsewhere.

All have extensive networks and partnerships on many levels with others in the UK and internationally – wherever the expertise happens to be – with individual researchers, academic societies, industrial and commercial companies and institutions.

To take just one example, the Division of Signal Transduction Therapy (DSTT) is a consortium devoted to drug discovery and development bringing together the research strengths of the university of Dundee and the Medical Research Council with the financial clout of six of the world's leading pharmaceutical companies: Astra Zeneca, Boehringer-Ingelheim, GlaxoSmithkline, Merck and Pfizer.

The two key co-directors' working lives demonstrate the depth of these knowledge networks. Professor Sir Philip Cohen worked in

London and Seattle and his colleague Professor Pete Downes worked at the MRC in Cambridge and at ICI in Cheshire.

These national and international networks centred on life sciences at Dundee have assembled over 700 scientists and support staff from 56 countries. The team leaders have overwhelmingly worked in other UK institutions and the pace has undoubtedly accelerated in the last decade.

The overall evolution of the Scottish economy over the last ten years shows how our comparative future growth increasingly depends on knowledge creation and dissemination through key networks. Services are up from 64 per cent in 1995 to over 72 per cent in 2003. And Scotland's move towards a high value economy has continued apace since the creation of the Scottish Parliament.

Apart from education, the fastest growing sectors between 1995 and 2005 were: telecommunications (at almost 350 per cent); banks, building societies (over 100 per cent); business services (nearly 90 per cent) and air transport, insurance and pension funds (over 70 per cent).

So, increasingly Scotland's comparative advantage comes from our ingenuity and inventiveness. An economy making the necessary transition and using its greatest asset of all: its people and their creativity. It is an economy which works against those who tell you we will be stronger apart and weaker together. The truth is that for all nations and regions of the UK we are stronger together and weaker apart.

It is in fact the best strategy for Scotland: to combine the flexibility which devolution gives in taking account of local conditions and strengths with the benefits we have identified from partnerships and macroeconomic stability within the UK.

Conclusion

This year we mark the 300th year of the United Kingdom. The Union in 2007 is now clearly founded on social justice. We pool our wealth to ensure that every part of the Union has the resources it needs to meet its social, economic and geographical demands.

Yet within the powers of our own parliament at Holyrood, elected representatives can decide how those resources are used. The Union has made us part of the fourth largest economy in the world. And the rest of Britain is Scotland's biggest market.

Breaking up the Union means breaking these trading links which have seen 200,000 more Scots in jobs since 1997 and more Scots in employment than ever before. Scotland is a country advancing towards full employment instead of a country weighed down by high unemployment and its social consequences.

But the SNP's politics of grudge and grievance refuse to recognise these realities. They have to explain why Scotland would want to stop being part of one of the most successful union of nations in history.

We have examined here the strong economic case for union. But our Union it is not only about economics. Socially, our Union has been one of the most successful in history. A million Scots live south of the border – more than three quarters of a million people who live in Scotland were born in England. Half of us have relatives in England and people throughout all parts of the UK move freely to set up home.

25

The Nationalists have to explain why those we call family should instead be called foreigners.

Politically, our Union gives Scotland – and Britain – a powerful international voice. It allows us to lead debate in the European Union on economic and social reform which is good for Scottish jobs and good for Scottish workers' rights. And the challenges which Scotland and Britain face which demand greater partnerships – not isolation.

These challenges – climate change, international terrorism, poverty – require collective action, not just between individuals and governments, but between nations. Scotland can be take every necessary measure to protect our environment but it will have little effect on our climate if we do not join with our neighbours in England, Europe and countries across the globe to make a real difference.

Partnerships between nations, open markets and political and economic co-operation are not just desirable in this new young century, they are prerequisites. They say all politics is local, but if Scotland is to stand tall in this ever changing world then we have to look at our politics from a global perspective. The nations making most progress in the world are those which are learning for themselves the lesson of our history – that partnership drives us forward, and borders hold us back.

The 21st century demands that countries, cultures and peoples across the globe learn to work together. How then can it be that the countries, cultures and peoples of these small islands, woven so closely together over the last three hundred years in the Union, cannot now live together and instead have to rip apart what generations have freely built?

When the SNP look at Scotland they do not see reality. They do not see the confident and prosperous nation which we are, they do not see a country which lives in partnership with its neighbours, they see one which lives in their shadow.

They do not see what Scotland is – alive and contributing to the international community – they see us as dependent on London. They do not see a Scotland which is happy to play a part on the world stage.

Their reaction to the G8 summit in Gleneagles and the Make Poverty History campaign sum up their lack of vision.

While most Scots are proud that history was made when world leaders came here and signed the deal to cancel debt and double aid to the poorest nations on earth, the SNP complained about who paid for the Police.

The challenges which Scotland faces in the 21st century – which all nations face – require us to exploit every advantage we have to the maximum. Being part of the United Kingdom is one of our most important ones which it would be folly to throw away. This is not a static union but one which has evolved and which will continue to evolve. Working in partnership with our nearest neighbours is one of the keys to our success.

The Nationalist case is essentially one of past centuries and not of this one. Instead of revelling in old arguments, our national test is to face up to the challenges of the future and of the knowledge economy.

If Scotland is really to stand tall in the world, the arguments at May's election should be about how Scotland makes sure her people have the skills and education to make the most of themselves and their country in that global knowledge economy. A future defined by constitutions and divorce can only divorce us from the realities of the 21st century.

In truth, the Union is about more than a constitution. It is a message to the world. A message which says that nations of different traditions and identities can live harmoniously and prosper with a common purpose.

Fabian Review

www.fabians.org.uk
Spring 2006

What do they
really think
about equality?

Inside this special equality issue

Meg Munn and Bob Niven on Labour's equality programme.

Louise Bamfield asks whether the Tories have changed.

Jenny Watson predicts a new alliance of men and women.

Richard Brooks and Sunder Katwala on life chances.

Stella Creasy on the equality of local participation.

Melvyn Bragg remembers Phillip Whitehead's life.

Ed Miliband and Kitty Ussher recommend equality books.

Tom Hampson sets out Britain's equality opportunity.

Tired Britain

Michelle Harrison presents new data revealing the inequalities of everyday life.

The trickle-up effect

Stewart Lansley on how the undeserving rich are getting richer.

The quarterly magazine of the Fabian Society   Volume 118 no 1

£4.95

The Fabian Review, Spring 2006

Featuring: the rise of
the neoprogs

Fabian Review

www.fabians.org.uk

Summer 2006

THE WORLD AFTER BUSH

In this global issue

Sadiq Khan on being a
British Muslim

Jack Straw on increasing
Labour Party membership

Andrew Jones on what's
been achieved since Live 8

Nick Pearce on Francis
Fukuyama's neocons

Hannah Jameson on Joe
Klein's *Politics Lost*

PLUS:
Ed Balls in Gaza

The quarterly magazine of the Fabian Society   Volume 118 no 2   £4.95

Gordon and Hillary

Wishful thinking? Brian Brivati
on the special relationship

Interview:
Paddy Ashdown
returns home

Tom Hampson asks about
Blair, Bush and whatever
happened to 'the Project'?

Nicky Gavron

50 years on from the Clean Air
Act, the Deputy Mayor asks if we
can tackle climate change like
we cleaned up London's smog

The Fabian Essay

*"On a bright, cold day in
January as the Washington
clocks strike twelve, you
might just, if you listen care-
fully, be able to hear a
swooshing sigh of relief as it
travels around the world. As
the 44th President of the
United States takes the oath
of office at noon on the 20th
January 2009, George W
Bush's Presidency will enter
the history books.."*

Read **Sunder Katwala**, p17>>

The Fabian Review, Summer 2006

Fabian Review

www.fabians.org.uk

Autumn 2006

BRITAIN AFTER BLAIR

LABOUR CONFERENCE SPECIAL

SO WHAT NEXT?

JOHN DENHAM
CHARLES CLARKE
DEBORAH MATTINSON
SUNDER KATWALA
ANTHONY GIDDENS
LOUISE BAMFIELD

The Fabian Profile
Can Ségolène save France? The
dream of a Royal presidency.

The Fabian Essay
Roy Hattersley on why Labour's next
generation need Crosland.

PLUS: Five things our new prime minister needs to know about women voters

The quarterly magazine of the Fabian Society   Volume 118 no 3   £4.95

The Fabian Review, Autumn 2006

Fabian Review

FABIAN CONFERENCE SPECIAL

www.fabians.org.uk

Winter 2006/07

TEN MORE YEARS

BUT WHAT WOULD HAVE TO CHANGE?

The next decade
Five challenging essays on foreign policy, education, life chances, democracy and the environment.

The Fabian Interview
Balancing Westminster and west Yorkshire. A day with Yvette Cooper in Labour's heartland.

The quarterly magazine of the Fabian Society   Volume 118 no 4   £4.95

The Fabian Review, Winter 2006

'The Fabians ask the most difficult questions, pushing Labour to make a bold, progressive case on taxation and the abolition of child poverty.' **– Polly Toynbee**

How can we make poverty history at home?

One in five children still grows up in poverty in Britain. Yet all the political parties now claim to care about 'social justice'. This report sets a litmus test by which Brown, Cameron and Campbell must be judged.

'Narrowing the Gap' is the final report of the Fabian Commission on Life Chances and Child Poverty, chaired by Lord Victor Adebowale. The Fabian Society is the only think tank with members. Join us and help us put poverty and equality at the centre of the political agenda.

How to break the hospitals' grip on the NHS

In this Fabian pamphlet, **Dr Howard Stoate MP** says that the Government's future NHS vision will fail if they cannot find a compelling public argument which can win locally against the 'save the hospital' brigade.

Challenging the Citadel: Breaking the hospitals' grip on the NHS sees health select committee member Dr Stoate and Bryan Jones argue that the NHS is far too focused on the hospital as an institution.

The new NHS should be about public health and health prevention, and if the dominance of the hospitals continues we will find ourselves unable to make substantial improvements in health outcomes, and the NHS will be ill-equipped to cope with the pressures it will face in the 21st century.

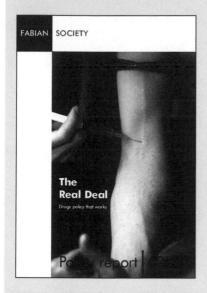

FABIAN SOCIETY

**The
Real Deal**

Drugs policy that works

Policy report

The Real Deal: a drugs policy that works

In the Fabian policy report *The Real Deal: Drugs policy that works* the senior backbencher **John Mann MP** set out the case for a radical overhaul of UK drugs policy.

Mann argues for a new approach to drugs classification, and for compulsory drugs treatment for addicts involved in crime. He says that "coercion should be recognised as not only legitimate but necessary to get users off chronically addictive drugs such as heroin" and says that concerns about civil liberties are misplaced because "free choice" is meaningless for serious addicts.

The report's recommendations seek to address the links between drug addiction and crime, based on work done in John Mann's Bassetlaw constituency where the decision to treat drug use as a medical problem massively reduced drug-related crime.

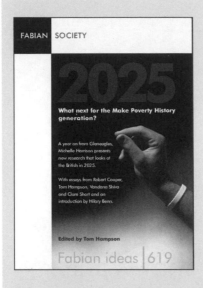

Will the Make Poverty History generation lose its commitment?

Britain came a long way between Live Aid in 1985 and Live 8 in 2005. The Fabian pamphlet *2025: What next for the Make Poverty History generation?*, edited by **Tom Hampson**, asks what the next twenty years could hold.

What positive vision for 2025 is needed to keep the British public mobilised? Despite Live 8, individualism is now stronger than community.

For the first time since 1994, according to our Henley data, a majority of people says that looking after ourselves is more important to quality of life than looking after our communities.

Hilary Benn, Robert Cooper, Tom Hampson, Clare Short and **Vandana Shiva** set out their own visions of global change and the politics needed to make them a reality.